THE GULLS OF SMUTTYNOSE ISLAND

THE GULLS OF SMUTTYNOSE ISLAND

words by Jack Denton Scott

photographs by Ozzie Sweet

G.P. PUTNAM'S SONS NEW YORK

Library of Congress Cataloging in Publication Data
Scott, Jack Denton, 1915–
The gulls of Smuttynose Island.
Summary: Describes the life of herring gulls and great black-backed gulls on Smuttynose Island,
one of the two largest gull rookeries along the New England coast.
1. Gulls—Juvenile literature.   2. Birds—Maine—Smuttynose Island—Juvenile literature.
[1. Gulls]   I. Sweet, Ozzie.   II. Title.
QL696.C46S38   598.3′3   77-7870   ISBN 0-399-20618-3

Second Impression

FROM A GULL'S VIEW AT FIVE THOUSAND FEET, THE
clouds running below look like a vast mountain range, billowing and
misting and weaving through space. Far below, through that shifting
cloud vapor, what resembles an eighteenth-century flotilla seems to be
beating against the waves.

These, however, are not ships cresting the wind-foamed water, but the famous Isles of Shoals. At the turn of the century some of them were exclusive summer resorts; now they are mainly a natural paradise for gulls and other seabirds.

Two of the islands, Smuttynose and Appledore, are the ranking gull rookeries along the New England coast. Nine in number, with a total of 205 acres, the isles, Appledore, Cedar, Duck, Malaga and Smuttynose are part of Kittery, Maine. Londoners, Seavy, Star and White belong to Rye, New Hampshire.

But if possession is nine tenths of the law, the gulls virtually own Smuttynose and Appledore. The birds could not have selected a more perfect location if they had gathered in council and planned it. Ten miles out in the Atlantic Ocean from Portsmouth, New Hampshire, lying within a quadrangle 3 miles by 1.5 miles, these two among the nine glacier-scarred granite-domed islands are exclusive gull mating, breeding, nesting and training grounds. They are also nurseries, battlegrounds, and cemeteries for these unique birds of the sea that have made them theirs.

Appledore, with its 95 acres, is the largest of the islands. Once called Hog Island because its rounded hill was said to look like the hunched back of a hog wallowing in brine, it was elevated to the status of a township in 1661. At that time all of the isles were given the blanket name of Appledore after the village of Appledore near Portsmouth on the southern shore of England. Only this isle retains the name today.

The 28-acre Smuttynose took its unusual name from a black smutch, a natural discoloration of the stone, on its rocky profile at the southeastern edge. Smuttynose is the more private of the two islands. It is unoccupied, with a lofty look to the sea, a prime place for the gulls that will keep returning to the island of their birth as long as they live.

Beginning in late April, the gulls move northward in flocks to these breeding grounds. But unlike geese, the flocks are not necessarily composed of families or related colonies. No one is certain where all the gulls come from, for their range is vast, covering the Atlantic coastal waters from Florida to the Arctic. Their winter range extends southward to Bermuda, the West Indies, Texas and the Yucatán, and on the Pacific coast from British Columbia south to Mexico.

Flying from 35 to 50 miles an hour, gulls sometimes make a migration of 800 or more miles in 24 hours. Only geese, some ducks, hawks, and homing pigeons can match this record.

One morning as a sailboat rounds the outside curve of Smuttynose in the warm spring sunshine it sights the advance echelon of gulls that has suddenly arrived, a few bobbing on the sparkling water, others poised on the long tongue of rock that juts into a cove. Like an advance guard sent to see if the island is ready for their arrival, a half dozen gulls stand on a rocky promontory, sea spray misting around them. Others leave the water and stride along the rocks on an obvious tour of inspection. These gulls are for the most part the familiar herring gulls and the larger black-backed gulls, the two species that make up the largest part of the gull population on Smuttynose.

Only a few hours later, as the same sailboat completes the circle around Smuttynose, the gull population has grown considerably, for the birds have dropped from the sky unnoticed, gathering on the island's rocky edge nearest the sea, then carefully moving inland. Like anyone who migrates to the south for the winter and returns north in the spring, the birds are checking their summer place to see if it wintered well, moving from rock ledge to rock ledge and niche to niche.

Now there is a dramatic arrival—a sudden flurry of wings as a small flock of laughing gulls visiting on their way farther north drops down to the cove from a considerable height, as is their custom, and wades ashore, a few at a time. These black-hooded birds are in spring- and summer-breeding plumage. When they return south to winter, their heads will be white with grayish markings.

Laughing gulls are noted for their thieving fishing techniques. They will hover in the air, graceful as swallows, while pelicans dive and catch fish. When the pelicans surface with fish in bills, they must open their mouths to let the water drain before they swallow their catch. Swiftly the laughing gulls swoop down, perch on the pelicans' heads, snatch the fish, almost as a single motion, and fly away crying "*half, half, half,*" a sound much like sardonic laughter, from which they got their name.

About half the size of herring gulls and the great black-backed gulls that are now arriving in considerable force, the laughing gulls are also much less aggressive. The laughing gulls will stay only long enough to rest and to fish for crabs in the shallows and small fish near the surface of the water. They will be joined briefly by Bonaparte's gull, a smaller, black-headed bird; the kittiwake; and the ring-billed gull, gulls that also make the island a temporary stopping place. The laughing gulls will eventually fly up the New England seacoast to breed and nest on an island largely populated by terns.

The gulls' Smuttynose is a historic island. Settled by Samuel Haley in late 1700, the important breakwater was built by the founder's son, Captain Samuel Haley, Jr., in 1820 from the proceeds of four silver bars which he found under a flat rock. Captain Teach—"Blackbeard" the infamous pirate—spent his honeymoon on Smuttynose and is believed to have hidden considerable gold and silver here.

Here, also, some Spanish sailors met a tragic fate. It was Captain Haley's custom to place a lighted candle in the window of his cottage (circa 1750, it is said to be the oldest house in Maine) for the benefit of sailors. On the night of January 14, 1813, the Spanish ship *Conception* out of Cadiz was storm-driven upon the rocks off Smuttynose. Fourteen sailors made it to shore, saw the far-off gleam of the candle in Haley's window and tried to walk to it through blinding snow. But they were lost in the huge drifts. Not one survived. Later Captain Haley buried the unidentified sailors, and their graves were eventually marked with granite tombstones.

From the peak of the roof of the old Haley cottage, gulls today scream away the ghosts of seamen and pirates making their own presence and residency loudly evident.

As if proclaiming their ownership by representation, a pair of greater black-backs and a pair of herring gulls stand upon a rocky ledge, a symbol of the summer to come when one thousand pairs of greater black-backs and six thousand pairs of herring gulls will inhabit Smuttynose and nearby Appledore.

Day by day the gulls take over, perching high on the ancient rock formations of which one island is made. They even claim the lichen-and-seaweed-covered rocks exposed when the tide is out. They roost on the spray-lashed ledges in the cove, the water-surrounded rocks near shore, and stand sentinel-like on the cliffs that face the sea.

They coast self-confidently through the moonlight over to Appledore and settle on the roof of a seaside cottage, long empty. Morning finds the aggressive black-backs on the shorefront sign of Cornell University's marine laboratory, which is the only activity, other than the gulls, on the island. A herring gull makes itself at home on the laboratory's tractor, and a squadron lines up on a house facing the lighthouse on White Isle. Others perch on another shadowed cottage abandoned to the memories of the past when Appledore was a lively, status-starred place where luminaries such as James Whitcomb Riley, Harriet Beecher Stowe, James Russell Lowell, Nathaniel Hawthorne, John Greenleaf Whittier, Henry Ward Beecher and Ole Bull, the famed Norwegian violinist, spent the summer months.

Returning to Smuttynose at dusk, the gulls find a friendly fisherman who pays a tariff for anchorage on their land. Unafraid, they swoop in to take a tidbit from his hand.

Although it may seem so to the occasional human visitor, the gulls we are observing do not devote most of their time marking out or proving their ownership of Appledore and Smuttynose. Indirectly, perhaps one reason for their blatant self-confidence is that invisible mantle of protection that has been dropped over them by federal law. Killing any gull is punishable by a fine of $500 and six months in jail.

It wasn't always so. Less than a century ago the herring gull (the most populous) was almost wiped out along the North Atlantic coast. Gulls' eggs were sold by the barrelful; market hunters shot them by the thousands for milliners who used the birds' snowy feathers and black-trimmed wings to spruce up ladies' hats. At the end of the nineteenth century the gulls were so rare that adults were selling for 50 cents apiece.

That slaughter was finally stopped when intelligent observers noted that the herring gull seemed to prefer the debris of civilization to anything else. Here was an effective sanitation department that worked without wages. It required time, but eventually the gull's appetite actually saved it and the other gulls in the United States. The herring gull took all the other species along with it when the law was passed protecting gulls.

It doesn't take a bird expert to identify any gull. The overall appearance of gulls is much the same, differing mainly in size and coloring. Most species are white, one is gray, some (as we have seen) have black heads. Immature gulls are a dusky brown. The Soviet Union has a pink gull, and also recently announced the discovery, at Lake Ala-Kul in Siberia, of a rare colony of solid-black gulls. Male and female look alike, except that the male is larger with a thicker beak. All are built like graceful sailplanes, with each wing ranging in size from twelve inches to over three feet.

All gulls are members of the *Charadriiformes* species and the *Laridae* clan. Of the forty-four recognized species, twenty-nine breed in our northern hemisphere, some carrying names as stirring as their flight— Aden, Chinese blackheaded, Magellan, Patagonia. The most widely distributed of all birds, a species of gull can be seen, at least part of the year, in every state.

The name "sea gull" that many of us lump all species under is a misnomer. Gulls not only have the most interesting names in the bird world, but also do well away from the sea, some species preferring dry land. Franklin's gull not only migrates straight across the equator to spend its winters south, but also is so often found in wheatfields and prairies that ranchers in the western states call them "prairie pigeons." During spring plowing these gulls flock behind the plows and gobble grubs and worms. Franklin's gulls are respected by the farmers for their ability to wipe out infestations of grasshoppers, cutworms and other harmful pests.

The garuma, or gray gull, nests in the deserts of South America, and the ring-billed gull is often seen a couple of thousand miles inland, for it prefers fresh to salt water. It flocks and breeds in the vicinity of the Great Lakes and, like the Franklin's, is frequently seen during the spring and the fall in freshly plowed fields.

The two species of gulls described in this book, although closely related and with similar habits, have one dissimilarity. The herring gull (so called because it gathers in flocks to dive and feed upon schools of tiny herring, often driven to the surface by savage bluefish), with its mantle of pearl-gray, is often seen near populated areas. The great black-backed gull, with the ebony saddle that gave it the name, prefers solitude.

But both have come to Smuttynose for the same purpose: to breed in a natural, protected breeding ground used by themselves and their gull ancestors for many years.

Territorial imperative is the law at Smuttynose. The black-backs are larger (28 to 31 inches in length, with a 5½-foot wingspread, compared to the herring gull's 22½- to 26-inch length and 4½-foot wingspread) and therefore select the higher reaches of the island, the pinnacles of rock and the knolls. This forces the herring gulls to keep to the lower areas closer to the water. Black-back guards patrol their territories, both land and aerial, and fiercely drive off the herring gulls that try to trespass.

But it is not all the rights and rules of trespass. Each gull, no matter where it is—in the air, on the shore, alone or in a group—is a member of an exclusive club system that dates back more than a million years.

Each spring, when the gulls return to Smuttynose, the black-backs and the herring gulls re-form the private clubs, by species and by status. A small gullery of about two-hundred birds would have as many as four clubs. The huge population at Smuttynose probably has one hundred such clubs, formed for the social life and preservation of the species. The bringing together of the clubs each spring begins with a gigantic parade, with all of the birds joining in a walk around the rookery. Next comes a concerted flight, swooping and circling over Smuttynose and nearby Appledore, where most of the gulls were born.

The signal for the re-formation of the clubs begins when one old, aggressive bird glides from the parade in the sky and stands alone, head raised. At this signal, all birds descend to land, and what seemed a formless collection of gulls is converted into a series of close social circles, ruled by class distinction. Each club has its leader, an old, aggressive male, with several "associate" males just a step farther down in the status-by-age-and-aggression scale. The clubs annex their own terrain where the birds always gather in groups when they are not mating, breeding, nesting, flying or on food forays. Once these clubs are formed, the birds belong to them for life.

Like all clubs, these have their newcomers, brought in by other club members. There are clowns and playboys, young birds that pretend to pick fights, and swashbuckling swains that flirt with the older females, as well as the unfortunate members of every club that the other members harass.

Most of the older birds returning to Smuttynose are mated, but the younger ones reaching their fourth summer eagerly search for mates. Usually the female is the aggressor in the matchmaking, often cooing soft, melodious calls, sidling up to the male of her choice and pressing against him. If he ignores her, she reaches up and gives him a sharp peck

on the head. This develops into a chase with her fleeing on the shore and in the air over land and water, with spectacular aerial acrobatics. When they finally glide down and land, the lengthy billing and cooing begins; the nudging, the touching of bills, the placing of bills within each other's open mouths.

Sometimes the courtship evolves into a dance, the gulls facing each other, necks outstretched, bodies tilted forward, wings fluttering, the birds moving as gracefully as ballerinas. During the dance both birds utter low-pitched sounds, not unlike water gurgling from a bottle.

After being approached by a female, fluffing his feathers to make himself appear larger, and glaring around at other males, the male will sometimes regurgitate food before the female. This bribe, which if accepted by the female eating part of the offering, means that the mating will be consummated. This often is the procedure after the described chase, although sometimes the food is offered without the frenzied activity of the chase and the "capture" ritual.

Courtship can be further complicated when a fickle female approaches four likely males within two minutes, moving from one uninterested male to the next until she recognizes the response she is seeking and becomes aggressively acquisitive.

Once that mating is consummated, however, it is for life. But that also is a complicated and somewhat puzzling situation. For example, these perfectly matched pairs of black-backs and herring gulls, in their sparkling white breeding plumage, may have arrived at Smuttynose in different flights. For, while they are gone from their summer place wintering in the south, the pairs separate.

Although gulls may migrate in flocks to the same areas of the south and even live together in colonies as they do on Smuttynose in the spring and summer, their winter lives are drastically different. They migrate along the seacoasts where food is more accessible. Some stop longer than others. Each bird appears to go more or less its own way.

Niko Tinbergen, the world's foremost herring-gull expert, says that in the winter the gulls never show any behavior indicating personal attachment. "A winter flock," he claims, "seems to be made up of individuals, not pairs."

Once they return to Smuttynose, it is as if they had never parted. As Tinbergen observed, "The pair keep strictly together, and when they move from one area to another they are attached to each other as if by a string." This ornithologist saw one pair in flight instantly recognize each other at the summer breeding place at a distance of thirty yards. He later observed many more proofs of this amazing power of recognition, mates identifying one another at great distances and in various positions.

With the noisy and somewhat frenzied courtship completed, the birds begin accomplishing their purpose for returning to Smuttynose: breeding.

That ritual is performed with much stretching of necks, tossing of heads and lifting of wings. The males utter hoarse, rhythmic calls before mounting the females in the act of copulation.

Immediately after the series of deep calls, the male leaps onto his mate's back, fluttering his wings, his feet resting on the female's upper wing, which his toes are gripping. She continues tossing her head, twisting it around and rubbing her bill against his breast. Still making his deep calls, the male lowers his tail until it touches hers, then makes a number of sideways rubbing movements. Finally he brings his tail down at the side of the raised tail of his mate. Beating his wings to keep his balance, he then brings his cloaca into direct contact with hers for fertilization. This is repeated as many as seven times. Then the male ceases his coarse cooing, folds his wings and gracefully jumps down beside the female. Both birds immediately begin a busy preening of feathers.

Shortly afterward the couple, which will now remain paired until one dies, begins a careful search for a nest site. On Smuttynose this means the selection of an ideal formation of rocks, a ledge among bushes, a deep, protected niche, or a natural cupping of rock. Once found, they march around the chosen site, inspecting it from all angles. Consisting of from five to ten square feet, it becomes their territory, which they protect with vigor.

Both birds begin collecting twigs, moss, discarded feathers, seaweed and grass for the nest. The male is the major worker, but he defeats his own purpose by opening his mouth and "mewing," thereby losing part of the nesting material each time he carries it toward the site.

When the nest has been partially formed, they take turns sitting in it, picking up and rearranging material while in the nest and restlessly turning in all directions—with a purpose. The constant adding and rearranging, and the movement while in the nest, results in a well-rounded, well-lined nest-cup about eighteen inches in diameter and four inches thick.

Days before she lays the first egg the female hovers over the nest as if she were incubating eggs. Days later, when she does lay the first egg, there is an abrupt change in the daily rhythm of the pair. Prior to this, the birds were together continually, at their club, in the air, on the flights for food. Now, although the first egg is rarely incubated, it is always guarded by one of the pair because other gulls will eat the egg if given the chance.

At intervals of two, often three, days the other eggs are laid. The normal clutch is three greenish or bluish eggs about the size of chicken eggs, speckled with chocolate, black, or purple spots. The spots break up the contour of the eggs, helping camouflage them against the neutral background of the nest.

Now the incubation begins in earnest. Both gulls take turns sitting on the eggs, with a bird occasionally leaving the nest for a period rarely exceeding ten minutes, and only if its nest-relief is late, which seldom happens. Gulls are serious incubators, so much so that if the female arrives early to spell the male, often he will not leave the eggs until his incubation-clock tells him to do so.

The eggs are warmed constantly by one parent or another and turned about seven times daily for even heating and incubation. The embryos will develop properly in twenty-four to twenty-eight days, with the average twenty-six days, when the first egg that was laid is hatched. A day or so prior to this, however, the incubating birds appear to grow impatient, restless. Two days before the shell of the first egg is piped or broken through, a weak peeping comes from the nest, prompting the bird to climb off, stand beside it and, with head cocked, look down at the egg, presumably the one from which the peeping is coming.

Mere hours before that first egg hatches, a rock-hard calcium deposit grows on the tip of the tiny beak of the chick in the egg—its life-giving "egg tooth." Using that hard tip, the chick strikes the wall of the shell. Tiny cracks first appear near the large end. After trying all day, the chick manages to break a small hole, but the struggle for freedom is only beginning.